Data Analytics and Python Programming 2 Bundle Manuscript

Beginners Guide to Learn Data Analytics, Predictive Analytics and Data Science with Python Programming

Series: Hacking Freedom and Data Driven (Junior Edition) + Data Analytics

By Isaac D. Cody

DATA ANALYTICS AND PYTHON PROGRAMMING

2 BUNDLE MANUSCRIPT

Beginners Guide to Learn Data Analytics, Predictive Analytics and Data Science with Python Programming

ISAAC D. CODY

QUICK TABLE OF CONTENTS

This book will contain 2 manuscripts from the Hacking Freedom and Data Driven series. It will essentially be two books into one.

Data Analytics will help you learn how to leverage the power of data analytics, data science, and predictative analytics.

The Junior Edition will enhance your python programming skills whether you have past experiences in Python or just starting out!

Data Analytics:

Practical Data Analysis and Statistical Guide to Transform and Evolve Any Business

Leveraging the Power of Data Analytics, Data Science, and Predictive Analytics for Beginners

BY: ISAAC D. CODY

DATA ANALYTICS

PRACTICAL DATA ANALYSIS AND STATISTICAL GUIDE TO TRANSFORM AND EVOLVE ANY BUSINESS

Leveraging the power of Data Analytics, Data Science, and Predictive Analytics for Beginners

ISAAC D. CODY

attempt has been made to provide accurate, up to date and reliable complete information. No warranties of any kind are expressed or implied. Readers acknowledge that the author is not engaging in the rendering of legal, financial, medical or professional advice.

By reading this document, the reader agrees that under no circumstances are we responsible for any losses, direct or indirect, which are incurred as a result of the use of information contained within this document, including, but not limited to, —errors, omissions, or inaccuracies.

Preview of this book

Have you ever wanted to use data analytics to support your business?

With many businesses, data analytics can just that plus more. It's a great system to see how things are going, and you can collect the information to form conclusions through this. But how does it work? What are the nuances of this? Well, that's where this book comes in.

In this book, you'll learn the following:

- What are data analytics

- The importance of big data

- How to conduct data analytics

- Why a business needs this for success and prosperity now, and in the future

With data analytics, you can save your business, and this book will further prove to you the importance of this subject, what it can do for you, and how you can use data analytics to make your business shine and grow

Table of Contents

Introduction

I want to thank you and congratulate you for downloading the book

Data Analytics: Practical Data Analysis and Statistical Guide to Transform and Evolve Any Business, Leveraging the power of Data Analytics, Data Science, and Predictive Analytics for Beginners

This book contains proven steps and strategies on how to become proficient with big data, data analysis, and predictive analytics, even if you have never studied statistical science. This book takes you from the beginning concepts of data analytics to processing the information, structuring your organization, and even security issues with data management. From the knowledge contained within this book the business owner can create and install big data analytics in even the smallest business.

Data analysis has been proven to change the business world. Companies that are using data analysis for their business decisions are moving ahead of the competition by leaps and bounds. Armed with the knowledge supplied from their analysts, business owners and organizations are making better business decisions regarding marketing, sales and forecasting, to name just a few helpful functions of data analysis.

Here's an inescapable fact: you will need data analysis to keep up with the competition, because they are using it now, in real-time, to make their business decisions.

If you do not develop your understanding of data analysis and big data, you will be left behind in the dust. Your sales may drop and your business may be in jeopardy as a result of inexperience and the lack of information about a growing and necessary trend in business intelligence.

This book is an amazing resource that defines data analysis and the tools and methods that make it successful.

Good luck!

Chapter 1   The Importance of Data Analytics and Why Your Business Should Use It

Data analytics is the buzzword of the decade. Everyone is discussing and promoting data analytics from healthcare to big business. Small business and mega-corporations are touting the advantages of using Big Data to transform their business practices. Warehouses, trucking companies and suppliers are raving about the money they have saved using Data Mining to overhaul their organizations. Is it hype or is it the new Casino, offering cash at every pull of the slot machine handle (or in this case, the data set)?

Data analytics (DA) is the process of interpreting raw data for the purpose of informing the individual (or group) the conclusions derived from the data. Data analytics are used throughout industry to make business decisions on inventory, cash-flow, sales projections, customer characteristics, and loss-prevention strategies, just to name only a few of the practical uses. In science, data analytics are used to prove and disprove theories.

The concept of business analytics and big data has been around since the 1950s to predict insights and trends in the consumer markets. The difference between data collection sixty years ago and today is that today's information set is almost in real time. Today businesses can receive the information in thirty minutes or less to make an immediate business decision. This gives companies that use data analysis a big competitive edge over a company that does not.

The data that is received today by a corporate executive is thorough, fast and reliable. This allows the decision maker to determine the best course of action within minutes of receiving the desired information, rather than weeks, months or even years as previously experienced.

Businesses are tapping into the data mines to utilize the information in many ways, including, but not limited to:

1.   **Cost reduction for data storage**. In 1981 it cost $700,000 to store 1GB of information. In 1996

that cost was $295.00 and in 2014 that same storage cost was only $00.03. (*source:* http://www.mkomo.com/cost-per-gigabyte-update)

2.   **Opportunity for real data for R&D.** Customers are now very vocal about their wants and needs. A new product launch on Twitter can determine quickly the interest in an innovative product design. Data analysis allows immediate feedback for research and development of market trends.

3.   **Inventory and product analysis.** Using data analysis, a company can see what is popular on the shelves and what products need dusting off and moved on out of the store and off the valuable shelf space. Why do grocers' place the most utilized products on the very top and very bottom shelves? They know those products will always sell but the products with the highest markup are at eye-level for the consumer.

Lenovo was designing a new keyboard for their customers, but failed to recognize their loyal customer base in the gaming industry. After using data analytics, Lenovo changed their design to incorporate the gamers' needs and launched a worthy product that brought millions in sales. Data analytics saved their product and increased their profits.

Data analytics is by no means limited to the retail sector. Other businesses use data analytics to increase their profitability and efficiency. Here are a few uses that are currently being adopted by industries:

Travel and Hospitality

Customer satisfaction is very hard to measure but the key to a thriving enterprise. Big data analytics give the management instant access to customer preferences as they check-in, at customer decision points, and even as they leave the facility. This gives management the opportunity to rectify grievances as they occur, turning a potential customer relations bomb into a satisfactory experience for all parties concerned.

Health Care

In the health care industry, big data is changing the way records are kept, research is analyzed, and patient care is managed. The result is a better method of caring for the patient with a computerized record that can follow the patient no matter treatment is given. In addition, sometimes a new procedure or medicine is available immediately because of the instantaneous information of a query. Staffing for hospitals has been transformed also with data analysis, allowing the care facilities to schedule more personnel in the peak times and less for the slower times.

Government

Local police forces are using data analytics to determine the areas with the greatest crime statistics, where more foot patrols would be advantageous, and even the peak times for burglaries and petty crimes. The technology of analysis can pinpoint the problem areas in a suburb or city without sacrificing the limited manpower for surveillance.

Small and mid-size businesses have the same opportunities for collecting data as large factions, but it will be helpful to keep in mind these strategies:

To tap into the mainstream of consumers there must be a digital presence for the business. Customers and clients that are shopping for services and products go to websites and Social Media for opinions, reports, comparisons and reviews.

The website should be straightforward and honest. It should also describe the benefits of the product or service without exaggeration or misrepresentation. Consumers know hype when they see it, and will studiously avoid those websites as potential outlets of information or products. The website should be enabled to give information and to collect information.

Website analytics will gather the demographics of the customer, their interests, their entry point, their boredom and "click off" point, and their favorite social media sites.

If the website is designed correctly with many points of interaction, the client or customer will specify their needs and wants before they realize they have been "mined".

Small Business Example

Here is a good example of a small business that used big data:

A local bakery finds the chocolate chip cookie sales are booming, with orders by the dozen on both the website and from call-in orders. The chocolate cupcakes, however, become slower and slower to move. The baker reads the remarks on the website and finds this innocuous remark: "I love the chocolate cupcakes and the chocolate chip cookies, but I can buy 12 chocolate chip cookies for the price of only 2 cupcakes."

This data became an "aha" moment for the baker. The baker quickly made a separate page for just cookie sales (to continue the chocolate chip cookie trend), but also changes the product offering of full-sized cupcakes to mini-cupcakes. Four mini-cupcakes were priced the same as the chocolate chip cookies by the dozen. The baker also placed a coupon special on the Facebook listing of "buy one dozen assorted cookies and receive a free mini-cupcake of your choice, by mentioning this ad." Sales of all cookies and the new product increased.

23

Chapter 2   How to Handle Big Data

Big Data and Its Issues

Big data is the data mined that is too large, disorganized or unstructured for an analysis using the traditional technology and techniques currently used in data management. The quantity of data is less important than the how the data is used and categorized.

Big data is divided by three sectors: volume, velocity and variety. Companies are inundated with huge amounts of data and need ways to identify and utilize the data sets.

Regardless of the management issues, big data is still very valuable for a business or organization. Big data makes information transparent and usable. Now that organizations are collecting larger amounts of data, it is much less expensive to store in digital formatting than it ever was by tape. Management uses performance data to explore trends in sick days and employee tardiness, product inventory, movement, and even storage capacity. Other businesses are using data to explore forecasting for budgets and purchasing decisions.

Big data aids companies in segmenting their customer base so that they can tailor the product offerings to the customer needs and desires. More importantly, big data is being utilized in Research and Development to improve the next generation of service and product offerings.

Grabbing and Grasping Big Data

Companies now have to use new storage, computing, collecting, analysis and techniques to capture and crunch the big data. Even though the technology challenges and even the priorities of individual firms are different, they all have the same issues: older computer systems, incompatible formats, and incomplete integration of data that inhibits the interpretation of the database information.

There are new approaches available for crunching the data to assist with quality management of big data. The best approach will analyze the volume, variety and complexity of the data before making purchasing decisions.

Big data has open source technologies for the database management systems, including Hadoop and Cassandra. There are also several business intelligence software products on the market that report, present and analyze the finished product to the business owner.

Utilizing Big Data for Business

It is estimated that businesses only use 5 percent of the information they receive. This leaves a big space for improvement, which may be filled with the technological stack of implements needed for Big data analysis. There is a requirement of storage, computing, visualization software and analytical software, to start the list. There will the need for additional personnel and probably an IT department.

Does investing in big data payoff in the ROI? In a nutshell, positively. The McKinsey Global Institute anticipates that a business that correctly utilizes big data could increase the operating margin by over 60 percent, a huge sum.

Here are the steps suggested to implement big data in your organization:

- Inventory all data related assets

- Move the management to embrace a data-driven worldview

- Develop technology implementation

- Address policy issues including data security, privacy and property

- Identify opportunities and risks

Data security is of particular importance. Databases contain confidential information that may be trade secrets, personal medical information, and even copyrighted materials. Data should be centralized and secure. Encryption is not an option due to the large amounts of data and the time and personnel that would be required to continue such a practice. Protection of the database begins with the first step mentioned, inventory all sources of input. Only when the scope of the contributing sources is analyzed can businesses determine which security measures need revamping and which particular products with take care of the job.

Chapter 3   The Benefits and Challenges of Data Management

Long ago and far away the business owner would look at a new product, listen to the sales presentation from the jobber, and decide upon whether to purchase the product based on their "gut" intuition. Just like the general store with a post office and gas station, those days are gone.

This is the age of information. Businesses must keep current with trends, market dynamics, consumer preferences, and economic pressures to make the appropriate decisions regarding their presence in the marketplace. The enormous amount of information that is available requires educated persons that are comfortable and accurate in interpreting the data provided.

Case Western Reserve University in Cleveland has recently announced there will soon be a shortage of 190,000 analytics personnel and over 1.5 million data managers. This problem will mostly affect the small and medium sized businesses that cannot afford to hire a personal data analyst on a shoestring budget.

The demand for Information Technology Project Managers with big data skills increased by 123.6% last year, and big data skilled Computer Systems Analysts increased 89.8%, according to Forbes Magazine.

(source:
http://www.forbes.com/sites/louiscolumbus/2014/12/29/where-big-data-jobs-will-be-in-2015/#2caeda00404a)

Even when a business has access to data analytics there are still challenges for the business besides how to use the information provided. One of these challenges is Data Management.

Data management is the organizational management of the data and gathered information for security, limited access, and storage issues. Tasks that the data management requires include governance policies, database management systems, integration of data systems, data security, source identification, segregation of data and storage issues.

Keys to Effective Data Management

Data management issues are not a new dilemma. As long as data has been collected the businesses have been dealing with the problematic issue of keeping data pristine. Now, with the increase in data and marketing automation, data security has moved to the pinnacle of the problem areas.

If data isn't clean or relevant, it is of no use to the marketing and business primary officers. Data management requires constant surveillance as hackers are waiting to scoop up and destroy millions of relevant information and resources. There are few things that should be automatic for security issues with data, such as:

1.   **Limit Access**

Many times the access to materials and information is wide open to all employees to modify. Office managers, sales personnel, and office staff should not have the ability to enter the database and change, access or delete and add information. The best way to control this situation is to establish boundaries, or limited access.

Set controls based on specific functions, such as marketing personnel are limited to viewing market data, but not to editing. Determine which person in the organization will do all the data changes including additions/deletions and actions (such as changing contact information for the client). Establish data import and export rules so that secured data is not flying out the door and so that viruses are not being uploaded. Create a master list of data so that information is neither duplicated nor compromised.

2.   **Create a Data Map**

A data map is a flow chart data the route of data, delineating the intake and output, the departmental integration, and the use for each data entry. Data mapping is an ongoing exercise that maintains controls and data consistency.

3.   **Organize your Data in Segments**

Data is not about quantity but instead about quality. It does no good to have millions of names in the database if your clientele is in the hundreds. It is not helpful to have hundreds of names in the database if you have no organization for retrieval.

Instead, separate the data by your needs. Examples could be by sex, age, address demographics, zip code, contact preferences, etc. Correctly segmenting the database can make the data come alive with potential whereas a disordered database will look and feel like chaos.

Begin with your current active customer base. Segment them into demographics and then by purchasing habits. Connect with your customers on a regular basis to glean their input on your products and services.

4.   **Data Hygiene**

Data hygiene is the process of keeping data clean and current. Old data and corrupted data will only clutter your database and possibly even infect all of your records. Just like the previous functions, hygiene should be provided on a regular basis to ensure the data is not decayed or contaminated.

The importance of maintaining a pristine and organized database cannot not be overlooked. If the data isn't good, all the contacts and marketing projects will not succeed if they are addressed to the wrong contact point. To enhance the value of your database for marketing and sales endeavors, do not neglect database management.

Chapter 4   Real World Examples of Data Management

An Example of Ineffectual Usage

- John Belushi, 33
- Chris Farley, 33
- Jimi Hendrix, 27
- Philip Seymour Hoffman, 46
- Whitney Houston, 48
- Michael Jackson, 50
- Janis Joplin, 27
- Heath Ledger, 28
- Cory Monteith, 31
- River Phoenix, 23
- Elvis Presley, 42
- Prince, aged 57
- Anna Nicole Smith, 39

- Amy Winehouse, 27

Source:
http://www.usatoday.com/story/life/people/2016/06/02/celebrit
ies-who-have-died-addiction/85314450/

These celebrities have a sad connection: They all died from a drug overdose at a too young age.

The prescription drug-monitoring program can inform prescribers (doctors and nurse practitioners) and dispensers (pharmacists) to establish controls for drug abuse and diversion of opioids, the major contributor to the aforementioned deaths.
Celebrities only make up a small percentage of the yearly deaths attributed to drug overdoses. The US Centers for Disease Control and Prevention (the CDC) has established that it is the primary cause of accidental death in the United States. At the last published data analysis, it was determined there were over 47,000 drug overdoses in 2014. Prescription pain killers were responsible for 18,893 of those deaths.

Source:
http://www.cdc.gov/nchs/data/health_policy/AADR_drug_poisoni
ng_involving_OA_Heroin_US_2000-2014.pdf

The names of these drugs are common prescriptions when one has surgery or a broken arm or just about any circumstance that requires a trip to the local hospital emergency room: Percocet, Lortab, OxyContin, Fentanyl, Vicodin, Morphine and Xanax are just a few examples. Xanax is a benzodiazepine, not a painkiller, but is lethal when ingested with an opioid, even at the minimal quantity of just one dose.

For preventing this epidemic of drug overdose, the separate states have established databases to monitor prescriptions of the products. This database entails the dosage, the frequency the prescription is filled, and the prescribing doctor, in order to determine which patients may be diverting or mismanaging their dosages and which patients are frequenting different doctors and hospitals within a thirty-day period to acquire more drugs.

The concept is great: Have one database that combines the data from various and multiple sources of pharmacies and medical personnel to combat the issue. Unfortunately, the database has several problems that prevent effective management.

- Data is derived from multiple sources and is time-consuming and complex.

- The data is incomplete as many physicians don't take the time to consult the database. Although the installation of the system is mandatory in 49 states, only 22 states require compliance, and no one is monitored for conformity.

- There are too few personnel to conduct real-time analysis of the information. It is fed into the database but not retrieved effectively.

Leading Data Analytics at SAS Institute have addressed the issue in the report *Data and Analytics to Combat the Opioid Epidemic*. Their take is that the information at present is almost unusable.

Source: http://www.sas.com/en_us/whitepapers/iia-data-analytics-combat-opioid-epidemic-108369.html

With better analytics and interpretation physicians could develop improved treatment protocols, patient education and policy boundaries. For example:

- Physicians can compare their treatments with their peers to determine specific patterns of early drug addiction.

- Insurance and government payment systems can catalog the potential misuse or diversion, avoiding the expense costs of paying for fraud.

- Larger hospital and public health systems could develop better educational programs, treatment protocols and resource decisions.

- Pharmacies could compare their dispensing data to determine geographic overlap in abuse, among other factors.

- States could utilize the database for funding treatment centers by demographical information.

Combining and segmenting the data could work to alleviate macabre headlines by saving lives.

An Example of Effectual Usage

A famous mid-sized business owner found $400,000 by using Data Analytics. It seems that he had lost track 1,000 items of inventory, which was impeding his much desired cash-flow. The first day that he started his inventory, he saw the product that had not moved from the shelves.

He initiated a huge warehouse sale and sold the entire stock in one weekend, increasing his cash flow by $400,000. This more than paid for the implementation of the new database and peripherals. With the quick and decisive move to sell the new-found inventory, the company has utilized their data in a positive fashion with immediate results.

Previously this company had no IT department and did not have a POS system that traced product aging. He had money molding on the shelves. Once he had the database system installed, he was able to reduce older inventory by 40%, in addition to changing price points that were overblown, supplier costs, and profit margins. He also cleaned up the customer base with updated information, saving a substantial sum on postage and printing costs. With his new information, he can target the purchasers of the product to upgrade their sales rather than broadcasting mail to uninterested households. This company also uses their data to offer special discounts to their loyal and top customers, which generates income through upselling.

Chapter 5   The Different Types of Data Analytics

Big data is such a buzzword there is a misconception of what it is and what it does. The uses of Big Data are tremendous: fraud detection, competitive analysis, consumer preference analysis, traffic management, call center optimization, managing utility power grids, and managing warehouse and inventory, just to name only a few. Big data itself is problematic because it is the business intelligence code word for data overload.

There are three V's of Big data:

1. Too much data, or **volume**

2. Too much speed; the data is moving so quickly it cannot be analyzed, or **velocity**

3. Too much information from too many sources, or **variety**.

Even though the collection and assimilation of big data is daunting, the business intelligence that is derived from big data can aid a business immensely.

Four Kinds of Big Data Business Intelligence

There are four kinds of big data business intelligence that are particularly helpful for business owners:

1.   Prescriptive

2.   Predictive

3.   Diagnostic

4.   Descriptive

Prescriptive Analysis

Prescriptive analysis is the most valuable analysis because it informs the business what steps should be taken to improve the situation. The use of this data can be the beginning of change for the organization. Even though it is considered the most valuable, it is the least used as barely 3 percent of the organizations reported to use big data. Companies could use prescriptive analysis to give specific issues to isolated problems, such as in the health care industry and the problem of diabetes and obesity. Big data could identify the obese patients with both diabetes and high cholesterol, three contributing factors in the development of heart disease. These patients could be targeted immediately to initiate a four-fold attack on the risk factors through diet, diabetes education, exercise encouragement and cholesterol monitoring. At present, the issues are addressed by different specialists, if they are even addressed at all. Combining treatment strategies would be much more effective and the combination of information could be compiled through prescriptive analysis.

Predictive Analysis

Predictive analysis is the prediction of possible scenarios derived from the analysis of the information. This is usually in the form of a business forecast. This form of analysis looks at the past to foretell the future. For example, the business might look at the previous Christmas sales to predict the future Christmas potential sales for a particular product. Predictive analysis is especially useful in marketing and sales departments to mimic previous campaigns that were successful. Some businesses are using predictive analysis to examine the sales process, from customer introduction, communications with the customer, the lead to the customer, the sale to the customer, the closing of the sale, and the follow-up communications.

Diagnostic Analytics

Diagnostic analysis focuses on past predicaments to discern the who, what and why of a situation. This analysis can use an analytic dashboard, or widgets that help the reader see at a glance the information at hand. An example of use of diagnostic analytics could be examining a sales campaign or a social media marketing campaign. With the widgets, one could see the number of posts, the number of visitors, the quantity of comments and likes, the page views and the feedback from the customer. Seeing these analytics at a glance instead of paging through reports brings a faster grasp of the salient points of the data. Utilizing diagnostic analytics will explain the failure of a marketing campaign to increase sales of a specific product.

Descriptive Analytics

This type of analytics gives real-time data on the current situation. Instead of giving last week's or even yesterday's data, this information is happening now. An example of the usage of descriptive analytics is pulling the current credit report for a customer desiring to purchase a new car. Examining the past behavior to assess the current credit risk and predict the future credit profile would help the sales manager determine if the potential customer can or will fulfill the credit contract.

Big data analytics will bring certain value to a company for the ROI because it fills in the blanks regarding customer performance and product sales. By reducing the enormity of big data into manageable chunks of information, a business owner can make better business decisions regarding staffing, sales, profits, and product variances.

Chapter 6   They all Work Together: Data Management, Data Mining, Data Integration and Data Warehousing

The terms for Big Data are many; this section of the book identifies the most useful terminology when addressing the logistics of big data.

Data management. Data management is the process of placing restrictions on the access and quality of data that flows in and through and out of an organization. Restrictions may include limited access, security measures to prevent viruses and corrupted data, and maintenance issues.

Data mining. Data mining is the process of sifting through the data to extract patterns and relevant information to solve the current issues in the business. Using software, data mining will take all the chaos out of the voluminous data.

Hadoop. This is open source software (meaning it's free!) to store data and run discriminating applications on commodity hardware. It is key to sifting the multiples of data information that is bombarding the data sets. It is known for the speed for which it processes data.

In-memory analytics. By investigating information from framework memory (rather than from your hard plate drive), you can get prompt bits of knowledge from your information and follow up on them rapidly. This innovation can expel information prep and investigative handling latencies to test new situations and make models; it's not just a simple route for businesses to stay agile and settle on better business choices, it likewise empowers them to run iterative and intelligent examination situations.

Predictive analytics. Predictive analytics uses, statistical algorithms, machine-learning techniques and data to identify the predictive outcomes based on previous patterns of usage. It's about giving a best evaluation on what will happen later, so businesses can feel more assured that they're settling on the best business choice. The most common and basic utilizations of predictive analytics incorporate misrepresentation and fraud, risk management, operations management and marketing functions.

Text mining. In utilizing text mining technology, the business you examine text data from the world wide web, comments, articles and other text sources to uncover insights that were previously unseen. Text mining incorporates machine learning and language processing to evaluate and sort web documents like blogs, feeds, intelligence on competitors, emails, comments and surveys to assist the business in analyzing quantities of information and discover tangents and hidden relationships.

Data integration is the combination of adding new information and data to an old computer system while keeping the data both clean and uncorrupted in content. Moving data effectively has become a challenge for businesses in the following areas:

- **Data Needs**

o Delivering the correct data in the required format to alleviate the business needs is the primary reason for the integration of data. Every new source of data can impact the previous collection of information and systems to which it migrates.

- **Anticipating the Needs of the Business**
  o Data is not helpful if it is not available in a timely fashion. Integration must be adequate to manage both batches of information and real-time

- **Confirm all Data is Stamped with Pertinent Information**

  o Old systems did not time stamp or date activity in the server. For quick identification of the changes made to the data, the data integration needs to record this information.

- **Be Suspicious of All Incoming Data**

  - It is natural to anticipate data from other sources, but be suspicious that it may be infected or other corrupt. Scan everything that comes in for compatibility and integration needs.

- **Validate Customer Information**

  - Compare incoming data to the master database to confirm the customer database is correct and current.

- **Keep a History of Every Change**

  - There is always a need to backtrack changes sometimes for statutory compliance and often when integration doesn't work as anticipated.

- **Upgrade the Systems and Evaluate the Process**

  o Constantly look for ways the system may be deficient for your business needs. Upgrade the systems regularly to ensure you have the best possible solution to your data management and integration needs.

Data Warehousing. Data warehousing is the storage of electronic data by the organization for which it is prepared. Data must be stored so that it is reliable, uncompromised, secure, easily retrievable and easily managed.

Chapter 7   Conducting Data Analysis for Your Business

We have stressed throughout this book the need for data analysis in the business enterprises, but we have yet to explain exactly how to collect data. This chapter will focus on basic data collection so that you can implement a strategy that will further your organizational goals.

A Step by Step Guide

What is Collecting Data?

Basically, gathering collected data implies putting your configuration for gathering data into operation. You've chosen how you're going to get data – whether by direct perception, interviews, overviews, investigations and testing, or different techniques – and now you and/or different spectators need to actualize your arrangement. There's more to gathering information, be that as it may. You'll need to record the information in suitable ways and sort the data so it's ideally helpful.

The way you gather your information ought to identify with how you're wanting to dissect and utilize it. Despite what strategy you choose to utilize, recording ought to be done simultaneous with information accumulation if conceivable, or soon thereafter, so nothing gets lost and memory doesn't blur.

Some of the functions necessary for useful data collection:

Assembling data from all sources.

Computing any numerical or comparative operations expected to get quantitative data prepared for examination. These might, for example, incorporate entering numerical perceptions into a diagram, table, or spreadsheet, or figuring the mean (normal), middle (midpoint), and/or mode (most every now and again happening) of an arrangement of numbers.

Coding information (deciphering information, especially subjective information that isn't communicated in numbers, into a structure that permits it to be handled by a particular programming project).

Arranging data in ways that make them simpler to work with.

How you do this will rely on upon your design of research and your assessment questions. You may amass perceptions by the independent variable (pointer of achievement) they identify with, by people or gatherings of members, by time, by movement, and so on. You may likewise need to group the collected information in a few distinctive ways, so you can consider interactions and relationships among various variables.

There are two sorts of variables in data. An independent variable (the intercession) is a condition executed by the analyst or group to check whether it will make change and improve the situation. This could be a project, strategy, framework, or other activity. A dependent variable is the situation that may change as a consequence of the independent variable or intercession. A dependent variable could be a conduct or a result.

How Do We Examine Data?

Investigating data includes looking at it in ways that reveal the connections, designs, patterns, and so on that can be found inside. That may mean subjecting it to statistical operations that can let you know not just what sorts of connections appear to exist among variables and additionally to what level you can believe the answers you're getting. It might mean contrasting your data with that from different data sets (a control group, statewide figures, and so on), to reach a few inferences from the information. The point, as far as your assessment, is to get a precise evaluation so as to better comprehend your work and its consequences.

There are two sorts of information you will use, even though not all assessments will fundamentally incorporate both. Quantitative data alludes to the data that is gathered as, or can be interpreted into, numbers, which can then be shown and broke down mathematically. Qualitative data are gathered as descriptions, accounts, conclusions, quotes, understandings, and so forth., and are by and large either not ready to be reduced to numbers, or are viewed as more important or enlightening if left as narratives. As you may anticipate, quantitative and qualitative data should be analyzed in different ways.

Quantitative data

Quantitative data is collected as numbers. Examples of quantitative data include:

- Frequency (rate and duration) of specific behaviors or situations

- Survey results (reported behaviors, ratings of customer satisfaction, etc.)
- Percentages of people with certain characteristics in the demographic (those with diabetes, obese, with heart disease indicators, the education level, etc.)

Data can also be collected other than numerically, and converted into quantitative data that is ready for analysis. Compilers can assign numbers to the levels of emphasis of a specific behavior. For instance, compilers can enumerate the quantity of Facebook "likes" or "comments". Whether or not this kind of information is necessary or helpful is dependent upon the kinds of questions your data is meant to answer.

Quantitative data is converted to statistical procedures such as calculating the mean number of times an event repeats. These calculations, because numbers are exacting, can offer definitive answers to varying questions. Quantitative analysis can identify changes in dependent variables that are related to – duration, frequency, timing intensity, etc. This allows comparative analysis with like issues, like changes within the population count of a zip code, or purchasing changes between women of a similar age.

Qualitative Data

Unlike numbers, qualitative information is considered "soft" data, meaning it can't be reduced to a specific conclusion. A number may indicate the population in a demographic, but the soft data may tell you the stress levels of the shoppers by the attitude and appearance of the customers.

Qualitative data can occasionally be converted into numbers, by counting the number of times specific things happen, or by assigning numbers to levels of importance, customer satisfaction or whether a function is user friendly when placing an order on a website.

The translation of qualitative data into quantitative data is dependent upon the human factor. Even if the customers agree to use the numbers 1-5 (1 being very unsatisfied and 5 being extremely satisfied) to evaluate customer satisfaction, there is still the issue of where 2, 3, and 4 fall on the assessment scale. The numbers only give a partial assessment; they give no information about the "why" of the customer rating. Was the customer unhappy because of the product inventory on the shelf, a detail about the product, a problem with the atmosphere or music in the store, the location of the store, etc.?

Likewise, when counting specific instances of a behavior, did the counter include those who exhibited only partial behaviors (those that hit "like" but did not comment on Facebook, for example)?

Qualitative data can impart particular knowledge that is not available in quantitative data, such as why a sales campaign is working, or how the campaign is culturally conflicting with the customer base. (In 1962, Chevrolet was puzzled why their new "Nova" was so popular in the United States but had almost no sales in Mexico. Researchers failed to translate the word "Nova" into Spanish, which means "no go." The Spanish vernacular for the name of the car was "doesn't run." No wonder sales were down in Mexico! The automobile was renamed to Caribe and sales increased.)

It is often helpful to evaluate both quantitative and qualitative data sets.

What are the steps to collecting and analyzing data?

- Clearly design and define the measurements that are required to answer the questions.

- Conduct the research for the needed period of time in the correct timeframe.

- Organize the data dependent on the function of the data; how will you use the information?

- If possible and appropriate, change qualitative data into quantitative data.

-

- Use graphs and visualization charts (examples are in Chapter 10) to make the data easier to assimilate.

- Visually inspect the patterns of information to identify trends and connections.

- Seek patterns in the qualitative data, just like the quantitative data. If people consistently refer to similar problems, these may be crucial to understanding the problem and a workable solution.

Interpret the findings by using one of the following categories:

- Your marketing plan is performing on target with no obvious problems.

- Your marketing plan had no significant effect on sales.

- Your marketing plan had a negative effect on sales. (Possibly it was offensive or deemed silly by consumers.)

- Your marketing plan had mixed results. The promoted product sold well but a previously popular product may have decreased sales. For example, Secret deodorant offered a new scent category that was very popular but the unscented product sales decreased significantly as loyal users just swapped their preferences.

- If the analysis shows your marketing program is working you have a simple choice of continuing the program or tweaking it to hopefully increase sales.

- If analysis shows the program isn't working, interpretation is more convoluted. What is missing from the equation? What factor is preventing the desired results?

Analyzing and interpreting the results brings you full circle in the process; now you can use the knowledge you've gain to adjust your business and improve your service. Continuing to analyze and evaluate the business goals and results will keep the business current and an effective presence in the marketplace.

Chapter 8 An Organizational Approach to Data Analytics

This chapter discusses the framework that needs to be in place in the organization that incorporates big data into the corporate culture. A workable analytics governance will enable the business to utilize big data for an edge over the competition.

The Framework

To integrate information technology, business intelligence, and analytics four dominant questions must be under consideration:

1. Are analytics a key component of the business, in the same categories as finance,

sales, product development, research and marketing?

2. Are the appropriate personnel in place?

3. Do the personnel have the ability for deep knowledge of the business needs?

4. Is there a governance structure in place?

This framework is referred to as the CSPG framework.

- Culture

  o Does the business revolve around the data analytics or does analytics take a backseat to marketing, R&D, and sales?

- Staffing

  - Is there adequate staffing and is hiring of qualified staff a priority? Does the IT department work on a shoestring budget or do they have the proper resources to conduct big data analysis?

- Processes

  - If the analytics process is completed correctly, data can be traded with like organizations without fear of contamination, allowing multiple streams of information.

- Governance

o Governance is a new concept for businesses that have come recently to the table of data analytics. The governance needs a structure that encompasses people, structure, and salaries so that the IT department is not out of variance with the other departments.

Placement of the Analytics Function in the Business

There are three models for placement of the Data Analytics function:

1. Placing the analytics department in a central unit. The advantage of this location is that it is easy to obtain data, integration into the company culture is simpler, and the data retrieval is faster. The challenge for a centralized department can be the location

(as an add-on department it may be located away from the hub of decision makers), there may be confusion as to whom the department reports, and the data analysts may be so far away from the corporate culture that they cannot anticipate the business needs.

The second possibility is to decentralize the analytics and place analysts in each department throughout the company. This allows the analysts to focus on the business sector in which they reside. The challenge is to work together on company-wide projects that are not segmented and need all the analysts focused on one problem set.

2. The third option is a mix of the two previous scenarios. This places the analysts in a centralized location but also deploys analysts throughout the organization. This requires a very large staff of analysts, which

may be the biggest challenge for the business.

The Key Analytics

Analytics is composed of models, infrastructure and operations. The models are statistical or predictive or datamining that are originated from statistical data. Key to the analytics process is the building of the models, which is usually performed by the analysts or data scientists or statisticians.

Infrastructure is the software components, applications used and platforms utilized for data management, data processing and decision making. The processes connected to analytics infrastructure are data management, model deployment and multiple analytics that must be incorporated in the business operations.

Operation are the processes that create the data used for models and actions for business use. Data can be purchased, internal, external, or collaborative.

The Data Analytics team must identify the internal and external relevant data, manage the data, build the analytical models and introduce the models into the internal systems. Most businesses organize these functions thusly: The business department requests the model, the Analytics team constructs the model, the IT department supplies the raw data, and operations launches the model. This brings us to the why of analytics governance.

Analytics Governance

The three challenges that businesses face when extracting big data are:

1. Identifying the unique needs for which the data will be used

2. Obtaining the needed information

3. Deploying the analytics models into the organization

The analytics manager must have enough authority to negate these challenges. The structure of governance needs a mechanism for identification, communications and resolution of issues stemming from data analysis problems. The analytics manager also needs the flexibility to hire qualified and knowledgeable personnel.

Chapter 9 Data Visualization

Visualization is what makes data come alive to the reader. A list of information can be a struggle to try to translate into useable data; translating the groups of data into a manageable form is essential to help the reader differentiate between the important and the superfluous.

Using graphic designing software can draw notice to the key statistics, and by using visual images, can uncover hidden patterns and connections that might not otherwise be detected.

The following is a list of *__free__* data visualization software programs that are easily accessible on the web:

Chart.js

http://www.chartjs.org/

This program offers 6 different graphics HTML5, and is one of the most popular small-charting programs.

Dygraphs

dygraphs.com/

This is a JavaScript charting tool that is customizable, works with almost all browsers, and is used for dense data sets. It is mobile device and tablet friendly.

FusionCharts

www.fusioncharts.com/

FusionCharts Suite XT offers more than 90 charts, 965 data maps, and customizable, interactive business dashboard. FusionCharts is AJAX application-friendly and can be used with JavaScript API.

Instant Atlas

www.instantatlas.com/

Instant Atlas combines statistics with map data, which is very useful with demographic information.

Raw

raw.densitydesign.org/

Raw is customizable and available for modification, can be uploaded from the app to the compute, exported as SVG or PNG, can be embedded into the webpage, and offers vector-based images.

Tableau

www.tableau.com/

Tableau allows the user to drag and drop data to update immediately into real-time charts.

Timeline

https://timeline.knightlab.com/

Timeline gives a detailed analysis of events that offers a clickable ability to open the chart for more particularized information.

Visual.ly

visual.ly/

Visual.ly is a gallery tool and an infographic tool. With Visual.ly one can build stunning representations of data that are brilliant and easy to create.

Visualize Free

https://visualizefree.com/

Visualize Free allows you to upload your own data sets and build HTML5 interactive charts for visualization.

ZingChart

https://www.zingchart.com/

ZingChart is another JavaScript charting program that has interactive Flash and HTML5 charts, more than 100 selections for your data analysis.

Chapter 10 Using Social Media

Domo released the infographic of statistics for Social Media users in 2015. Here are the statistics showing the phenomenal increase in users.

In just one minute,

BuzzFeed streams 34,000+ videos

Instagram displays 1.7 million+ photos

Netflix streams 80,000 video hours

Vine streams 1,000,000 videos

YouTube has uploads of 300 hours of video

Facebook has more than 4.1 million likes for posts (this is not the same as posts quantity as everyone does not take the time to like)

Twitter has 347,000 tweets

Source: Domo, Data never sleeps

Obviously Social Media is now a major player for reaching consumers. A successful implementation of integration with social media and business practices can only enhance the opportunities for customer development. It would be wise for businesses to search for their products to find the answers to their tricky troubleshooting problems.

One of the often-neglected sources of information for a retail-related business is YouTube videos. Customers often make available videos that demonstrate how-to's that are not available in the product user manual. Sometimes Frequently Asked Questions writers are stymied at a little-known product failure. YouTube may have the answer that can be a solution if the Analysts engage in data mining.

Social Media Analytics

Social media analytics is using gathered information from blogs and social media websites to make a business more successful and more visible. Having an Internet presence is key to attracting younger generations of customers. Eighty-one percent of purchasers under 30 use the Internet to influence their purchases. A connection point to these purchasers is primary to business growth and development.

Social media analytics involves the practice of data mining, analysis of website information, data gathering, and utilizing the information for business forecasting and product shaping. The primary use of social media analytics is to evaluate customer responses to support marketing progress and customer service decisions. The second major use of social analytics is to get an edge over the competitor by maintaining a presence on the web. The third use for social media analysis is to gauge the customer sentiment regarding a product or service. The fourth use for social media analysis is to enhance the products by offering web only resources and discounts. The fifth use of social media analysis is for producing products that are contrary to logic (like runners pulling the lining out of running shoes because it makes their feet too hot) but desired by the consumer.

Social media analysis is similar to any other data analysis, but has specific needs to consider such as:

Form the hypothesis

Social media analysis is more about why something happened and less about reporting the event itself. Begin the analysis with of a circumstance or even with a question of why. Why did readers engage with this question but not respond to a similar survey on Facebook or Twitter? Examine the posting frequency and times you post. Are they optimal for your brand or product? For example, advertising for a food delivery would be much more effective at 5:00 than at 2:00 in the afternoon, as customers are hungry and tired when they leave work and want an instant solution to the dinner-hour dilemma.

Utilize the information to identify new ways of sharing information that attracts increased reader traffic. For example, Twitter now allows Vine videos to be embedded into posts. A hypothesis for testing would be: Does the new addition to Twitter increase traffic to the website or just entertain the readers more fully?

Move the Data to a Spreadsheet

Start with identifying trends and patterns on the spreadsheet. From this data you can extrapolate issues and variances for exploration.

Expand the Sample to Encompass as Much Data as you Possibly Can

Expanding the sample can be accomplished in many ways, but here are two of the possibilities: changing the end date of the sample, or tracking the competitors also.

Question the Results

It is easy to determine a false correlation when there is more data than one needs. Just like proof-testing, it can be a quick resolution by finding data to support your anticipated and desired outcome.

Continue to test the results to eliminate bias in the conclusions.

Tools to Help Manage Social Media

Posting to several social media outlets day by day is time consuming, but also necessary. Rather than devote several hours a day to maintaining social media updates, consider some of the following tools that take the drudge out of daily monitoring.

Here is a list of recommended tools to help the business owner complete the task in less time. Some of these tools are free, but most require a paid subscription.

Buffer, HootSuite, and Sprout Social

These tools allow you to log in one time and schedule the posts for the major social media outlets. You can perform more than one function at the same time, writing and scheduling a week's worth of posts, analyzing the efficacy, and sharing information.

SumAll, Social Express, Socialight

These programs send the data to you instead of you having to go to them for retrieval. You get to choose what reports interest you for your business.

Social Count, SharedCount, BuzzSumo

This program tracks your "shares" from the different URLs. You enter the URL and it spits out the "shares" per day, week and month. This saves time so that you don't surf from Website to Website seeking the information.

Social Media Strategies for the Business Owner

These are the most helpful tips for the small and medium business owner that is managing the business and the social media.

Use a business dashboard to consolidate your social media.

Complete all social media posts at the same time and schedule them ahead of time.

Watch the engagement of your posts.

Segment your audience for faster analysis.

Social media is here to stay and gets bigger and more complex every day. Managing social media is now essential to maintain a presence on the web. Businesses that are ignoring social media with their heads hidden in the sand like ostriches are losing the opportunity for a new income stream. Online sales of products are increasing more every moment. In one minute, Amazon has over 4,000 new customers purchase a product. A savvy business owner will want to tap that potential customer base as quickly as possible.

Social media analytics helps the business owner target customers that are already interested in the product or service promoted by the organization. With a little attention to the customer service needs of the consumer, a pathway may be discovered that opens the gateway for communication and sales through the Internet outlet.

Chapter 11 How Data Analytics Can Sustain any Business

The Age of Analytics has dawned and the Age of Aquarius has moved on. Organizations that collect, interpret, and act on the raw data they derive can change to the rapidly moving marketplace, and stay well ahead of the competition.

To use the data correctly and quickly, analyzing the data with these tools will bring clarity and innovative suggestions.

Begin with **Measuring**, determines which analytics will be most helpful for decision making within the firm.

Diagnose the problems that have occurred with customer satisfaction or product placement. Why has something happened in an adverse way? Data analytics can help you locate the specific issue for a satisfying solution.

Predict and Optimize to forecast changes and the potential consequences of the change. Use the "if"…"then" method of questioning. (If I make this change with customer service how can I then anticipate the reaction?) This analytical technique helps to determine the direction of the organization and the best route to sustain continued growth.

Operationalize, or placing the information into use by the front-line workers, sales staff, engineers, marketers, managers and the remaining decision makers. This is the transition from analysis to usefulness, leaving the laboratory and moving into real-world experience.

Automation is when the business managers use real-time information to make immediate changes in the organization. For example, in a grocery industry, couponing is a big money maker for both the customer and the grocer. The grocer moves the product but is reimbursed by the couponing agency, along with a processing fee based on the value of the coupon. The customer receives the product at a reduced price, and the product is usually a newly introduced item that would be considered a luxury item in a depressed economy. What happens, though, when the customer takes advantage of the retailer by purchasing all of the shelf stock of the product, leaving none for the following customers and creating an environment of disgruntled customers? The store manager immediately assesses the situation and applies a "3 coupons only per transaction" rule. Now the customer can still purchase the item but very few want to leave the checkout to make more than one transaction. The retail grocer has used automation to analyze the problem and create an immediate solution.

The last stage of implementation is **transformation**, when the business moves to a data-driven corporate culture, making business decisions based on current analytics instead of tradition or gut instinct.

How You Can Collect Data for Analysis Today

1.   Establish a digital presence that both gives and receives information. Before you can collect data you need a way like a social media outlet and an interactive website.

2.   Remember your goal is to receive, sort, and address the data you have collected from as many sources as possible, as quickly as possible so the data won't be stale or even unreliable. The more data you collect the more accurate your findings will be.

3.   Focus on the questions that need answers. It will be tempting to read and ponder everything, but that will defeat the purpose of collecting the data. Keeping the questions at the forefront of your mind will help you mine the customer intelligence for the necessary information to change your business practices into a positive spin.

4.   Engage with your customers through social media. Don't assume you know what they want. Give them plenty of opportunities to push the like button. This valuable button will target the customers' wants and needs much better than a formal questionnaire.

5.   Use Google Analytics and Alex to determine relevant information regarding your client base. They have easy-to-understand statistics on website traffic and SEO rankings. Use this information to cater to your clientele. Just changing a few keywords on your site can increase your traffic and move you to number one in the Google search engine, a prime place for attracting new customers and readers.

Conclusion

Thank you again for downloading this book, *Data Analytics: Practical Data Analysis and Statistical Guide to Transform and Evolve Any Business, Leveraging the power of Data Analytics, Data Science, and Predictive Analytics for Beginners*!

I hope this book was able to help you to understand and utilize data analytics to increase your business sales, marketing and efficiency.

The next step is to implement the policies and procedures that are presented in this guide to data analytics.

Finally, if you enjoyed this book, please take the time to share your thoughts and post a review on Amazon. It'd be greatly appreciated! Thank you and good luck!

Hacking University: Junior Edition. Learn Python Computer Programming from Scratch

Become a Python Zero to Hero. The Ultimate Beginners Guide in Mastering the Python Language

BY: ISAAC D. CODY

HACKING UNIVERSITY

JUNIOR EDITION

Learn Python Computer Programming from Scratch

Become a Python Zero to Hero. The Ultimate Beginners Guide in Mastering the Python Language

ISAAC D. CODY

Table of Contents

Disclaimer

Introduction

Thank you for downloading the book *"Hacking University: Junior Edition. Learn Python Computer Programming from Scratch. Become a Python Zero to Hero. The Ultimate Beginners Guide in Mastering the Python Language."*

Python is a powerful and highly recommended language for beginners for a variety of reasons. This book serves as a beginners guide for those that have never written programming code before, so even if the thought of programming is daunting this book can explain it in simple terms. We will introduce the process from the very beginning with actual code examples; follow along to learn a valuable computer skill that can potentially land you a job working with the elegant Python language.

Related Software

For enhancing your Python skill, use an IDE. If you have not downloaded it yet, Atom is highly recommended for Python programming. Atom is customizable, in that you can install add-ons at any time to make programming easier. "autocomplete-python" is one such add-on that can guess what you are typing and automatically fill in the rest of the command.

VI and Emacs are two other popular text editors for programmers. Both are considered highly advanced and optimized for writing code, but a bit of a "flame war" exists between fans of both softwares. For the Linux Python programmer, investigate the two text editors and test whether it helps with Python workflow.

After you have finished a particularly useful Python program and wish to distribute it to users, you have to keep in mind that many of them do not have Python installed and will likely not want to install it just to run your program. PyInstaller (http://www.pyinstaller.org/) is a piece of software that builds your Python script and the needed modules into an .exe file that does not need Python to run. It is a handy software should distribute your applications.

Online Resources

For obtaining online help related to Python, you can always check the online documentation (https://www.python.org/doc/). The documentation contains examples and manual pages for every function built-in to Python and its included modules.

For times when programming code just does not work, you can always turn to search engines to resolve your problem. Typing in the error text into Google can turn up other programmers who also had the same problem and posted online. If the problem cannot be fixed by observing other code, websites such as Stack Overflow (http://stackoverflow.com/) are notoriously helpful in resolving code issues. Make an account their and post your problem politely and somebody will probably help you out.

Finally, there are websites that offer tutorials online about how to learn intermediate and advanced Python programming. http://www.learnpython.org/ is one particularly exemplary one, but the sheer amount comes from the fact that Python is highly used and well understood. For any time Python help is needed, a quick internet search may solve your curiosities.

The Job Market

As a popular language and because of its widely implemented use, Python jobs are abundant. Large companies and start-ups alike are looking for programmers that understand Python, and because Python is still increasing in use the jobs prospects will continue to increase.

Most companies do not require college education for programming jobs, because they understand that most programmers are self-taught. Obtaining a job in the Python job market is not difficult because of this, but it still requires preparation and dedication on the programmer's part. Younger Python programmers can gain internships at Google, Apple, Intel, and more just by showing a drive to learn. Adult Python programmers can apply for programming jobs by directly contacting companies or replying to job listings.

Search online in message boards, job sites, and freelance websites such as UpWork for prospects. Also ask around programming groups and attend job fairs to learn about companies that are hiring Python programmers.

Build a decent résumé and be prepared to prove your knowledge with the language. The interview process for programming jobs often contain "whiteboard" programming tests where you are presented with a situation and asked to use Python to solve the issue. They will not be too terribly difficult, but you certainly need to have a decent grasp on Python to pass.

Overall, finding a Python job is easy because of the current market, but also difficult because you need to know Python intimately. Dedicate yourself to applying for as many positions as possible and eventually a job will appear.

History of Python

Python is a programming language with origins in the late 1980's. Guido van Rossum, the creator, was looking to develop a language as a hobby project to supersede the ABC programming language. Taking cues from the popular C language, Python was created to be a powerful but easy to understand scripting language.

The term "scripting language" refers to the fact that written code is not actually compiled, but rather it is interpreted by an application. Normally this means that scripting languages are not nearly as powerful as actual programming languages. For Python, though, the opposite is true- the language remains one of the most powerful available for web servers and desktop clients. Development of Python continued throughout the 1990's until version 2 was released in 2000. The interpreter behind Python became intricate enough that current versions of Python are almost indistinguishable from lower level programming languages.

Throughout the mid 2000's and even now, Python continues to be developed by Guido van Rossum and a team of dedicated volunteers. The language gained great popularity due to its many benefits, and popular websites such as YouTube, Reddit, and Instagram even use Python for functionality. It seems as though Python will continue to grow for many more years as companies adopt the easy to use but highly useful Python language.

Why Use Python?

When first starting out learning how to program, the huge amount of options, information, and advice can be truly intimidating. Some experts claim that the difficult but time-honored C language is the best start, but other professionals say starting on an easier language such as Java or Python will give the learner a chance to actually absorb key concepts. Python is recommended for this exact reason-programming will not be as foreign and confusing by starting with a straightforward scripting language.

Python is easy to understand, an elegant and clean language, and free of many of the complicated symbols and markings that are used elsewhere. Often accomplishing a task using Python only requires a few lines of neatly formatted code.

Large companies such as Google, Disney, NASA, and Yahoo all use Python for their own programs; having Python knowledge could potentially land a programmer a job working at a high-profile organization. Moreover, because Python is continuously developed today with new features always being added, interest in the language will continuously increase with time. More companies will discover that Python is an exceedingly useful programming language, so learning it now will prepare you for the future.

Benefits of Python

In addition to being easy and fast, Python also has various other benefits. Python is very portable, meaning that Python code can run on a variety of different operating systems. Windows, Mac OSX and Linux distributions are all supported directly, and code written on one platform can be used on all of them.

Power is not compromised by Python's ease-of-use. The interpreter behind the scripting language is able to turn near-natural English commands into low-level processor instructions that put it on par with actual programming languages. Big-name companies choose to use Python because of this, and as websites such as YouTube and Pinterest prove, Python has a wide range of functionality.

Python is clean and retains a focus on readable code. Style and formatting are usually left up to individual programmers, but with Python neatness is absolutely required. For beginner programmers this instills good programming practices, which will dually help with Python and any other languages the novice wishes to learn.

Ease of development and testing also propel Python above other similar languages. Code can be run instantly with the interpreter which allows for rapid prototyping. Being able to quickly test out code means that bugs can be fixed quickly, allowing more time for other development goals.

Conclusively, Python is the perfect language for beginners. Both simple to develop for and learn, Python is also decently powerful. Fantastic for newcomers and those just starting out programming, Python remains the top choice of technology companies everywhere. Learning the language will prove to be useful now and into the future as its popularity continues to grow.

Setting up a Development Environment

Programming languages are typically used on Linux-based operating systems such as Ubuntu and Debian. Python is no exception, but there is another option of developing on Windows. This book will explain how to get both set up. It is important to know though, that we will develop with Python 3, rather than the older (but still extremely popular) Python 2.7.

Most Linux distributions actually come with Python installed by default. Therefore, there are no extra setup procedures to obtaining a working environment. The Python interpreter can be entered by typing "python" into a terminal console. If there are multiple versions installed, though, "python" will start the first one found. Check the version number in the interpreter, and if 2.7 launches you might have to type "python3" into the terminal instead. Press ctlr+c to quit out of the interpreter at any time.

Windows computers usually never have Python preinstalled. To obtain the software, navigate to the Python website and download the most recent version. As of now, Python 3.5.2 is the current version. So long as your version number is Python 3, the code written in this book should also be compatible. Install the software with mostly default settings. Definitely check the "Add Python to the Path", because it simplifies testing programs. After the installer is done the Python interpreter can be started by searching for "python" in the start menu.

The interpreter, or parser, is one of Python's advertised features that allows for individual lines to be written and run. For testing out code the parser is fantastic, but mostly every program we write in this book will be multiline, so we will need an IDE (integrated Development Environment). Windows has a few popular solutions, such as Atom, Pycharm, and Eclipse. These are all 3rd party applications that can be downloaded and installed. IDEs are essentially glorified text editors that offer helpful programming features such as syntax highlighting and command-completion. Although Atom is highly recommended for Windows developers, Python comes with an IDE solution already. IDLE is an interpreter program that can be made multiline by clicking on "file" and then "new file". Whether you choose to use the preinstalled editor or choose to get a full-fledged programming environment through Atom/Eclipse, the Python code will work just the same. You will write your code within one of the multiline programs.

On Linux you also have the option of downloading a Python-compatible IDE application, but most programmers tend to use the preinstalled application "nano". Nano is a built-in, barebones text editor accessible by typing "nano" into a console. The program can actually do some rudimentary syntax highlighting once it knows a Python script is being written, so many developers prefer the basic setup provided. Code is written into nano, then saved by pressing ctrl+x.

Now that there is a development environment set up, you can continue onwards to begin writing your first Python program.

Hello World

Mostly every programmer gets introduced to a new language by writing the "Hello World" program. Hello World is traditionally a simple exercise that involves displaying the titular text on the screen. To do it in Python, we must open up our IDE or text editor and simply type the function.

```
print ("Hello, World!")
```

Next, we save the file. In IDLE (and most IDEs such as Atom) one must go through "file" and click "save as". In Nano ctrl+x must be pressed. Name the file with a ".py" extension and save it in an easily accessible directory- your desktop is perfectly fine. For this demonstration we will name the file "test.py".

Running a Python file differs slightly between platforms. Windows must use the command prompt, while Linux must use the terminal. Open up the respective application (ctrl+R and then cmd for Windows, ctrl+T for Linux). These applications are text-based interfaces that can be used to navigate and interact with a computer. The printed line will tell which directory you are currently located in, and you can type "dir" in Windows or "ls" in Linux to display a list of files in that directory. Move to another folder by typing "cd" followed by the directory name. Since we have saved the file to the desktop, on both operating systems we can make it active by typing "cd Desktop". Finally, the Hello World script can be run by typing "python test.py" or "python3 test.py" (on Linux).

If the above programming code was copied exactly, the output "Hello, World!" will be seen. The program will run and then exit back to terminal/prompt. Not entirely glamourous, but a worthy first step into learning Python.

Programming Concepts

In the above program, "print" is referred to as a command or function. Each function has a specific syntax that must be followed. For example, after print there is a set of parenthesis. Values passed within parenthesis are called parameters. Quotations also surround our text, and that is syntax that specifies written text, or a string. The syntax of print must be followed exactly, or else a syntax error will be returned when the program tries to run. As new functions are introduced in this book, careful attention must be placed upon following the syntax rules.

Anything can be put within the quotations of the print function and it will be written to the console. Since Python starts at the beginning of a script and reads lines individually, multiple print functions can be placed one after another like so:

print ("Hello, World!")

print ("This is my 2nd Python Program")

print ("Notice how each print command puts the text on a new line!")

After saving and running the file, all three functions will print their respective parameters. As mentioned previously, the quotations explain that text will be displayed. By forgoing quotations, numbers can be displayed instead.

print ("The answer to everything is:")

```
print (42)
```

Python starts at the beginning of the script file and works its way down one line at a time until no more lines are found, in which case the program exits back to prompt or terminal.

Variables

Computers have the ability to "remember" data by storing the values as variables. Variables are RAM locations that are set aside to contain a value. Programming languages must specifically declare variables and assign them by writing code. Being able to manipulate data will prove to be a valuable asset when creating applications.

Creating a variable is known as "declaration". Giving a value is known as "assigning". Python simplifies the process by combining the two concepts into a single statement. Within a program the following line will create a variable:

```
lucky_number = 7
```

And then we can use the print function to view the variable we created.

```
print (lucky_number)
```

Because Python starts at the top of a program and works downwards, the above lines need to be in the correct order. If lucky_number is not first created, then print() will return an error for attempting to call a variable that does not yet exist.

An important distinction that can be made is seen when closely viewing the previous print() parameter. The variable lucky_number is not placed within quotations, so Python knows to print the value contained within (7). If we placed quotations around the text, Python would print "lucky_number", which was not our intended result. This situation is referred to as a logic error.

Variable Types

Variables can contain values of multiple types. Our first variable was assigned a numerical value, but Python has methods for handling values of different types as well.

```
secret_message = "rosebud"
```

```
print (secret_message)
```

As shown above, we can assign a string of text to a variable as well. The process is nearly the same, but notice the quotations around the value that explicitly indicate a string. Here are the most important data types in Python 3:

- Integer – Simple numerical value as a whole number.
  - 1, 0, -7

- Float – Decimal value. "Floating Point Number".
  - 3.0, -7.6, 1.0100001

- String – Letters, words, or entire phrases. Contained within quotation marks.
  - "Hello, world", "no", "12"

- Lists/Tuples/Dictionaries – Multiple related values grouped together as one object. Can be a variety of data types.
  - [1, 4, 4, 0], ["Dog", 2, "yes"]

Obviously, numerical values are declared by simply supplying an integer in the variable declaration. If there is a decimal involved, it will a float. Quotations signify strings, and brackets are for lists.

Variables can also be used in equations, or altered and changed mid-program. Write the following lines to a script.

first_num = 2

result = 3 + first_num

print (result)

```
first_num = 3


result = 3 + first_num


print (result)
```

      You can observe that the value 2 is assigned to first_num. Then, we create a new variable "result" that is equal to a short mathematical expression. 3 and 2 are added and assigned to the result, which is printed as 5. Then, first_num is updated to contain a new value. Result is calculated again and the new result is printed out. This program shows how easy it is to use variables within assignments, and how variables can be edited at any time in the program.

More arithmetic operations can be done to numerical variables by specifying an operator in the equation. The following list explains the 5 main operators and the symbol that is used to perform the sequence.

- Addition (+) – Combining numbers

- Subtraction (-) – Taking the difference of numbers

- Multiplication (*) – Repeated addition

- Division (/) – Grouping, or the opposite of multiplication

- Modulus (%) – Dividing and using the remainder as an answer

Both integers and floats can easily perform calculations using the above operators. Note, though, that integers will generally return integer answers (whole numbers) while floats will always return an answer with a decimal point. Python can usually transform an integer into a float when it is needed, but good programming form comes from choosing the correct data type at the appropriate time. For example, see how floats are used in the program below:

first_number = 5.0

second_number = 3.0

```
result = first_number / second_number
```

```
print (result)
```

And the console will return 1.666666 as an answer. Whereas if integers were used everything past the decimal would be left off for an answer of 1. Assigning the answer to the result variable is not entirely necessary in our small program, and we can rewrite it like so:

```
first_number = 5.0
```

```
second_number = 3.0
```

print (first_number / second_number)

String variables are not edited mathematically (as in 1 + "two" would not return 3). Instead, the remarks are changed by simply overwriting the words.

name = "Bob"

name = "Bill"

print (name)

Name will initially be created as the string "Bob", but "Bill" is assigned to it directly after. So when print() is called, the string only contains "Bill". Operators can be used, however, to combine separate strings.

my_string = "Hello,"

my_string2 = "World! "

print (my_string + my_string2)

print (my_string2 * 3)

The output would be "Hello, World!" for the first print(), and "World!

World! World!" for the second print().
The addition operator combines two
strings together into one massive string,
and the multiplication operator repeats
a string the specified number of times.

Input

Although what we have learned so far is interesting, predetermined applications are not very useful for the end user. Python allows us, though, to obtain input from the user to add a layer of interactivity within our scripts. The input() function assigns input to a variable.

favorite_number = input ("What is your favorite number? ")

When a program reaches this line, it will display the text specified and wait for user input. Whatever is input will be assigned to favorite_number, which can be called just as any other variable.

```
print ("Your favorite number is",
favorite_number)
```

Instead of using an addition operand, we use a comma instead. In print(), commas are used to combine multiple print statements into one (on the same line). We could have used either method, but operators cannot be used for differing data types. Both data types are strings in this case, so it all still works.

The answer that the user gives through input() will always be a string, though. If we were seeking a numerical answer we would have to convert it. Another function, int() can be used to extract numerical data from a string.

```
favorite_number = int(input ("What is
your favorite number? "))
```

```
print ("Your favorite number plus 2 is ",
favorite_number + 2)
```

There are a lot of new nuances going on in this program. For example, int() is used to convert the input into an integer. Notice how int() surrounds the entire input() function, which happens because input() must be passed as the entire parameter of int(). Next, the print statement is printing multiple bits of output, and the equation "favorite_number + 2" is evaluated before being printed.

Using int() will always return an integer answer, but float() could have been used to extract a decimal answer instead. The int() function works essentially by transforming the string "3" into the number 3. Definitely remember to include it whenever getting numerical input.

String Formatting

Being able to display strings with print() is useful, but sometimes our programs require us to display variables within them. To actually insert a variable into a string without first editing it or combining multiple variables, we can use a "string formatter". The format() function can be included within a print() statement to do positional formatting of variables.

dog_name = "Rex"

print ("My dog's name is {} and he is a good boy.".format(dog_name))

When you run the above code, it automatically replaced the brackets {} with the supplied variable. The format() is placed directly after the string it will be editing, and before the closing parenthesis. So when the code is run, the console outputs "My dog's name is Rex...". Without using format(), we would have had to use a multi-line complicated print setup. But format()'s greatest use comes from situations with multiple variables.

dog_name = "Rex"

dog_age = 12

print ("My dog's name is {0} and he is {1}. Sit, {0}!".format(dog_name, dog_age))

Here we choose to specify values within the curly brackets. 0 translates to the first supplied parameter, while 1 refers to the second variable. Therefore anywhere in our string we can use {0} to have dog_name be inserted and {1} to have dog_age be inserted. The console text will be "My dog's name is Rex and he is 12. Sit, Rex!"

Example Program 1 – project1.py

```python
user_name = input("What is your name? ")


user_age = int(input("What is your age? "))


user_pets = int(input("How many pets do you have? "))


user_GPA = float(input("what is your GPA? "))


print () #print a blank line
```

```python
print ("{0} is {1} years old. They have a
{3} GPA, probably because they have {2}
pets.".format(user_name, user_age,
user_pets, user_GPA))
```

This program combines what we have learned so far to obtain input from the user and display it back to them. A new concept, comments are introduced as well. The # symbol is used to denote a comment, or a block of text for human reading. Whenever a # is placed on a line everything after it is ignored by Python. Comments are used primarily to explain things to other programmers that might happen to read your code. In our case, we explain that a blank print() line simply produces a blank line. It is good programming form to use comments throughout your code to explain potentially confusing elements or help remind yourself of what certain blocks of code are doing.

Next, the format() function is used to replace 4 different instances within a print() function. As you might have noticed, counting begins with 0 in Python. 0 always refers to the first element of something, which is why 3 indicates the fourth supplied variable in our format().

Depending upon the medium in which you are reading this publication, some of the above lines may have word-wrapped to multiple lines. This is not how you should be typing it into a text editor though, as the print() line is one single command. Furthermore, copy and pasting from this document may introduce extra characters that Python does not understand. Therefore the correct way to input project 1's code is by typing it out yourself.

Homework program:

- Make a program that obtains information about a user's pet and returns it back.

Decision Structures

Now that the basics of Python 3 are explained, we can begin to offer truly interactive programs by implementing decision structures into our code. Decision structures are pieces of code (called conditional statements) that evaluate an expression and branch the program down differing paths based on the outcome. Observe the following example:

```python
user_input = int(input("What is 4 / 2? "))
```

```python
if (user_input == 2):
```

```python
    print ("Correct!")
```

```python
else:



    print ("Incorrect...")
```

    First we obtain input from the user. We test user_input against 2 (the correct answer). If the conditional statement turns out true, then the program will print "Correct!". However, if the user provides the wrong answer Python will return "Incorrect...". There is a lot of new concepts going on here, so we will break it down line by line.

    The first line is familiar to us; it obtains input, converting it into an integer and assigning it to the variable user_input. Line 2 introduces a new function- an "if statement". If statements are conditionals that evaluate the expression contained within the parenthesis. Our exact statement checks to see if user_input is 2, and if it is than the immediately following line of code is run. Comparisons use the "==" operator instead of the "=" operator. Double equal signs are checking for equality while single equal signs are only used to assign variables. Lastly, a colon follows the if statement.

Indentations are used extensively in Python to separate off blocks of code. Under the if statement is a tabbed line with a print() function. Because this line is tabbed in, it will not run normally in code. Rather, the line will only run if the conditional if statement is proven true. Because our user input 3 the conditional will evaluate to "False" and the "Correct!" line will not run. Instead the program moves on to the "else statement". Else is a keyword that means "run when the if statement fails". Another indented line follows the conditional, but this time the indented code actually runs because else becomes activated.

If the user had input the correct answer of 2 instead, the if statement would evaluate to true and the console would print "Correct". In that situation, the else statement would not run at all. Focus once again on the indented code and understand that those lines are indented because they are part of the "if" and "else" code blocks. Also realize that only one statement from a decision structure can ever run in a program, so if "else" runs, that means "if" did not run. Likewise a program that has "if" activated will not run the code block under "else". Conditional statements are not limited to single lines of code, as you can see below.

```
user_input =  input("What language is
this written in? ")
```

```python
if (user_input == "Python"):



    print ("Correct!")



else:



    print ("Incorrect...")



    print ("This is not written in {}, it uses Python!".format(user_input))
```

Another indented line is within the else code block, and both lines will run if the user does not correctly input "Python". This program does indeed compare strings, so quotations must surround the text.

Conditional Operators

Double equal signs (==) are only one of the many operators that can be used to create a conditional expression. This small list shows other operators in Python.

- \> - Greater than

- < - Less than

- == - Equal to

- >= - Greater than or equal to

- <= - Less than or equal to

- != - Not equal to

If statements evaluate whether the expression in the parenthesis is true; the above operators allow for some interesting expressions.

```
age = int(input("How old are you? "))
```

```
if (age <= 18):
```

```
    print ("Starting early!  Good for you!")
else:



    print ("Ah, a good age to learn.")



print ("Thank you for downloading this
book.")
```

A clever use of indentations is used here. If the user's age is 18 or under, it will congratulate them then skip the else statement and finally print out the thank you message. If the user is above 18 it will display the else message and then also thank them. No matter which conditional runs, the user will still receive the thank you message. The indentation makes all the difference about what code lines will actually run within a decision structure, and you must pay close attention to avoid a logic error.

For situations that require more than just two potential outcomes, the keyword "elif" can be used.

```python
age = int(input("How old are you? "))
```

```python
if (age <= 18 and age > 0):
```

```python
    print ("Starting early!  Good for you!")
```

```python
elif (age >= 80):
```

```python
    print ("Never too late to learn!")
```

```
elif (age > 18 and age < 80):


    print ("Ah, a good age to learn.")


else:



    print ("That seems like an invalid
age.")
    quit()



print ("Thank you for downloading this
book.")
```

Elif is a keyword that can be used to split the decision making process into multiple branching paths. Between if and else statements, any number of elif conditionals can be used. Also, another new keyword is used above- "and". Our first comparison checks to see if age is less than or equal to 18 AND greater than 0. Therefore that conditional will only evaluate to true if the age value satisfies both requirements. Pretend the user input 75. The first statement evaluates, and 75 is indeed greater than 0, but it is not also less than 18, so that statement is skipped. Then, the first elif is evaluated. Age is not greater than 80, so that statement is skipped as well. Thirdly, age is definitely between 18 and 80, so the console prints "Ah, a good age to learn" and then skips the else statement altogether.

Remembering that only one statement in a decision "tree" can ever run, we can see that any elif that activates essentially runs its code block and then breaks from the decision structure. Else is used as a "catch-all" type expression in our above program. Any invalid input, such as "-1" would be picked up by else and displayed as such. Good programming form comes from catching potential user errors like this, and as an aspiring programmer you should always be expecting the user to incorrectly input values whenever the chance arises.

"And" is a comparison operator that forces both parts of an expression to be true. Another operator, "or", is used to force only one part of the expression to evaluate to true.

elif (age == 25 or age == 50 or age == 75):

    print ("Happy quarterly birthday!")

If we were to put this elif within the above program (under the first if), we would see that only one part of the expression must be true for the whole comparison to be true. The user's age could be 25, 50, or 75 and the application would say "Happy quarterly birthday". Using "and" instead of "or" would be impossible, because the age cannot be 25 and 50 and 75 all at the same time. The keywords that we use for comparisons are helpful and greatly useful, but if used incorrectly they can lead to logic errors.

Example Program 2 – project2.py

```python
print("Python Quiz!")

answered = 0

correct = 0

print()

print("What version of python are we using?")
```

```python
print("A: 1, B: 2, C: 3")


user_answer = input("Enter A, B, or C: ")


answered += 1


print()


if (user_answer == "C" or user_answer == "c"):


    correct += 1
```

```python
    print ("Correct")


else:


    print ("Incorrect")


print()


print("How many 'else' statements can
be in a decision tree?")


print("A: 1, B: Infiniate, C: None")
```

```python
user_answer = input("Enter A, B, or C: ")


answered += 1


print()


if (user_answer == "A" or user_answer == "a"):


    correct += 1


    print ("Correct")
```

```python
else:

    print ("Incorrect")

print()

print("What does '=' do in Python?")

print("A: Compare, B: Assign, C: Both")

user_answer = input("Enter A, B, or C:
")

answered += 1
```

```python
print()


if (user_answer == "B" or user_answer
== "b"):


    correct += 1


    print ("Correct")


else:


    print ("Incorrect")
```

```python
print()


print ("You got {} out of {}
correct.".format(correct, answered))


if (correct == 3):


    print ("Congratulations!  Good
score.")


elif (correct == 2):


    print ("Good work, but study hard!")
```

else:

print ("Go back and read over the section again, I'm sure you'll get it.")

Homework program:

- Use if statements to create a calculator program that prompts the user for two numbers and an operator.

Loops

Just as conditional statements activate if an expression evaluates to true, looping conditionals also compare values in an expression. But while if, elif, and else statements are linear in nature, other conditionals have the ability to repeatedly run blocks of code. "Loops" are conditional statements that can be run several times through the course of a program, and they allow for expanded functionality within Python programs. A "while" loop is such a conditional.

```
answer = 0
```

```
while (answer != 2):
```

```
answer = int(input("What is 4 / 2? "))
```

```
print ("Correct!")
```

So long as the specified condition evaluates to true, the "while" code block will continuously run. We can see a perfect example of this through the program above. We create a new variable "answer" and repeatedly compare it to 2. While answer is not equal to 2, the program will ask the user for the correct answer. Inputting something other than 2 will just loop back around to the while statement, again prompting for the correct answer. If while finally does evaluate to true (because answer equals 2) the loop will break and the program will resume by printing "Correct".

The program can be enhanced further by "nesting" conditionals. A single indentation indicates a code block set aside for our while statement, but we can go for a second level of indentation to add an additional comparison.

```
answer = 0

while (answer != 2):

    answer = int(input("What is 4 / 2? "))

    if (answer != 2):

        print ("Incorrect...")
```

```
print ("Correct!")
```

This program uses "nested" functions to incorporate if statements within while statements. The sheer amount of possibilities gained from this are virtually endless. Note how there are indentation levels that determine which code blocks can run within which functions. Every intended block, both 1 and 2 indent levels, will run when the while loop activates. It is a hard-to-master concept, but one that surely increases functionality.

Another common loop is the "for" loop. For is different from while in that a for loop runs through a range of numbers or a set of values instead of checking a conditional.

```
for user_variable in range (1, 5):


    print (user_variable)
```

For takes the specified variable "user_variable" and uses the supplied range. The variable will be initialized at 1, and it will be iterated every time the function loops. By observing the output we can see how this works.

1

2

3

4

User_variable is printed out, then incremented to 2. It is printed again and incremented as 3. Once more time for 4. But it reaches 5 and stops, which is why 5 does not get printed out. Because the keyword "range" was used, the for loop will always start at the first number and stop at the second. Leaving it out will have the for loop cycle through the values given.

for user_variable in (1, 5):

    print (user_variable)

For example, only "range" is left out here, but the output is very different.

1

5

Python runs the loop with the first value, 1, and then runs it with the second value, 5. We will learn that using for loops this way is especially useful for lists, dictionaries, and tuples.

Lastly, loops can be broken with the break() function. Bad programming form can lead to infinite loops, but including break() as a safeguard might save a user's computer from crashing.

Example Program 3 – project3.py

```python
print("Adding simulator")

print("Type a number to add to total, or
type blank line to stop")

line = "a"

total = 0

while (line != ""):
```

```python
line = input("")

if (line == ""):

    break

total += int(line)

print ("Total = {}".format(total))
```

Homework program:

- Write a program using if statements that displays a text adventure game. Offer multiple choices to the player that they can type in to select. Use while loops to check the validity of user input.

More about Variables

       Lists are another data type beneficial to talk about. A list is an array of values that are grouped together into a single variable. The single variable can then be used to call upon any of the "sub variables" it contains. They are mostly used for organization and grouping purposes, and also to keep related variables in a similar place. List variables are created by initializing them.

state = "Texas"

jack_info = [8, "West Elementary", state, "A"]

```
print ("Jack goes to {} in
{}.".format(jack_info[1], jack_info[2]))
```

```
print ("He has a {} in math, even though
he's only {}.".format(jack_info[3],
jack_info[0]))
```

  The list "jack_info" contains four values because we specify four different entries between the square brackets. They are just ordinary values such as the integer 8 or the variable state, but they are grouped together for a common purpose by being placed into the list. As it is seen, entries in lists can be accessed by specifying the location of the entry in square brackets. Counting starts at 0, so the first entry of jack_info is 8, and the entry in [3] is "A". Visualize it like so:

Entry number:	0	1	2	3

Data value:	8	"West Elementary"	state	"A"

A list could be initially declared with 3 entries, and it would have the range 0-2. The number of entries is nearly infinite, and it is only limited by the computer's memory and the amount of variables the programmer fills it with.

The elements of a list can be edited as if they were individual variables. If Jack ages a year, we only need to update the entry. Furthermore, adding a new entry to the list can be done without completely redefining every value within it. Using append(), a new entry will be created in the last

state = "Texas"

```
jack_info = [8, "West Elementary",
state, "A"]



jack_info[0] = 9



jack_info.append(22)




print ("Jack goes to {} in
{}.".format(jack_info[1], jack_info[2]))




print ("He has a {} in math, even though
he's only {}.".format(jack_info[3],
jack_info[0]))
```

```
print ("Lucky number is
{}".format(jack_info[4]))
```

The new additions to the program change the list ever so slightly to now have a new set of values.

Entry number :	0	1	2	3	4
Data value:	9	"West Elementary"	state	"A"	22

Before continuing onwards, it is worthy to note a few more features about the string data type. Strings are actually lists that contain character values. As an example, take the string "Hello, World!". Broken down as a list, it would look like this:

Entry	0	1	2	3	4	5	6	7	...
Character	H	e	l	l	o	,		W	...

And likewise, individual entries can be displayed from the string list.

print (user_string[0]) # would print "H"

print (user_string[7:13]) #would print "World!"

Moving onwards, tuples are another data type within Python. They are declared by using parentheses instead of square brackets. Tuples are actually static lists, or lists that cannot be edited. They are used when the programmer needs to ensure a range of data cannot change.

jim_grades = (99, 87, 100, 99, 77)

print (jim_grades[2])

Notice how an entry in a tuple is still accessed using square brackets.

Dictionaries take the concept of organized variables and take it to an extreme. Just like lists and tuples, dictionaries can contain multiple values in a single variable. The difference, however, is that dictionaries organize their records through names instead of numbers. In this way, dictionaries are "unordered" lists of sorts, where any value can be called by the entry name. Declare a dictionary with curly brackets, separating out values with commas and colons.

pet_dict = {"Total": 2, "Dog": "Scruffy", "Cat": "Meowzer"}

print ("I have {} pets, {} and {}".format(pet_dict["Total"], pet_dict["Dog"], pet_dict["Cat"]))

Here, the dictionary pet_dict contains three values: "Total", "Dog", and "Cat". The entries are declared by naming the entry within quotations and then supplying a value. Those entries are called by specifying the name of the entry, such as with pet_dict["Dog"] to access the value stored within. An unprecedented amount of organization is available when using dictionaries because they resemble a database in form. Likewise, they can be changed, updated, removed, or added to at any time within a program.

```
albums = {"Milkduds": 2, "Harold Gene": 1, "The 7750's": 3}
```

```
albums["Milkduds"] += 1 #new album!
```

```
albums["The 7750's"] = 2 #actually only had 2
```

```
albums.update({"Diamond Dozens": 1}) #found new band
```

```
del albums["Harold Gene"] #sold one away, didn't like
```

```
print ("These are the number of albums
I own:")
```

```
print (albums)
```

The humorous example above is a simple dictionary used to store the number of albums a person has. At the beginning the dictionary has a set number of albums for each band, but the second line has the collector gaining a new Milkduds album. That line also uses a new code shortcut. Whenever "+=" is used, the code is actually expanded to be "albums["Milkduds"] = albums["Milkduds"] + 1", but much time and space is saved in the program by using the shorthand. Third line has the collector realizing they only had 2 7750's albums, so the command changes the value of the entry altogether. Next update() is introduced. It shows how an entirely new entry can be added to the dictionary. Sadly, though, Harold Gene is deleted from the dictionary because the collector sold away the album. Finally, printing the entire dictionary can be done by not specifying any entry.

A fun example, the above program actually shows how versatile dictionaries can be in gathering and storing data. Include them within your program to group variables together in an easy-to-call way.

Example Program 4 – project4.py

```python
keep_going = "a" #initialize variables
before they are used


number_grades = 0


grade_list = []


total = 0


print("Grade Average Calculator")
```

```python
print()


while (keep_going != "No" and
keep_going != "no"):


    grade = int(input("Enter a test grade:
"))


    number_grades += 1


    grade_list.append(grade)


    keep_going = input("Add more
grades? ")
```

```
print()
```

```
for x in range (0, number_grades):
```

```
    total += grade_list[x] #add up all
grades in list
```

```
print ("Average of {} tests is
{}".format(number_grades, total /
number_grades))
```

Homework program:

- Devise code for more math functions, such as medians and modes.

Functions

Every function used thus far has been built-in to Python and programmed by Python's developers. Functions are actually code shortcuts, as functions are condensed versions of code that take data as parameters, run longer blocks of code behind the scenes, and then return a result. The use of functions is to save time and code when doing commonly repeated tasks. Python retains the ability for programmers to write their own functions, and they are done like so:

```
def happy(name):
```

```
print ("Happy birthday to you. " * 2)
```

```
print ("Happy birthday dear
{}.".format(name))


print ("Happy birthday to you.")
```

The "def" keyword indicates a user
defined function declaration, and the
name immediately following is the name
of the function; we create the function
happy(). Within the parentheses are the
values that our function will take (only
one, a variable named "name"). Just as
print() must have a value, so does our
happy() need one too. Then, the code
associated with the function is indented.
Our code simply runs through a happy
birthday song, which supplying the
variable "name" inside the song. This
function declaration goes at the top of
our python program, but it does not
actually run when the program starts.
To call it, we need to specifically
reference the function in code.

```
happy("Dana")
```

Something interesting happens here. We call happy() by passing "Dana" as the value. "Dana" gets assigned to "name", and the function runs through. However, the variable "name" does not exist outside of the user defined function, and any attempts to call it will result in an error. This is because variables have scopes of operation, which are areas in which they can be accessed. "Name" has a variable scope that is specific to the function, so it will not ever be called outside of it. Similarly, any variables declared in the main program cannot directly be accessed by the user defined function, but rather they must be passed as parameters when calling the function. Follow along with the next exercise to see an example for an in-depth analysis on user defined functions (UDFs).

```python
def intdiv(num_one, num_two):


    whole_answer = int(num_one /
num_two)


    remainder = num_one % num_two


    print ("{} / {} = {} with {} left

over.".format(num_one, num_two,
whole_answer, remainder))



first = int(input("Enter first number: "))
```

```
second = int(input("Enter second
number: "))
```

```
intdiv(first, second)
```

First, the UDF is declared. This code does not run automatically because it has not yet been called. The program actually starts on the fifth line. The variable "first" is declared within the main program's scope based on the user's input. So too is the variable "second". The UDF "intdiv" is invoked with first and second as the two parameters. The variables are passed as parameters so they can be transferred into the UDF. First and second are not actually leaving their scope, though, because the UDF uses the variables num_one and num_two to perform calculations.

Variables can be passed back from a UDF by using the return keyword.

```
def exp (base, pow):

    orig_num = base

    for x in range (1, pow):

        base = base * orig_num

    return base
```

Above is a UDF that calculates the result of exponential multiplication based on two supplied values, the base and power numbers. The return keyword passes a variable back into the main program, which is how we can get around the variable's scope.

answer = exp(2, 3)

So when we call the function like above, the answer (base) is given back as the result and assigned to the variable "answer".

Conclusively, user defined functions can save a lot of time for programs that must repeatedly call a block of code. UDFs can just contain other functions, like our Happy Birthday UDF, or they can help simplify complicated code, such as our exponential multiplication UDF. You must remember that variables are defined within a scope that they cannot leave. However, values can be passed from the main program to a UDF by supplying them as parameters, and values can return from a UDF by using the return keyword and assigning the result to a variable.

Example Program 5 – project5.py

```python
def cm_to_inch(cm):

    inch = cm * 0.39

    return inch


def inch_to_cm(inch):

    cm = inch * 2.54
```

```python
        return cm


    print("Inch/cm converter")


    print("1: Convert cm to inch")


    print("2: Convert inch to cm")


    choice = int(input("Enter a menu
option: "))


    while (choice != 1 and choice != 2):


        print("Invalid, try again.")
```

```python
choice = int(input("Enter a menu option: "))



if (choice == 1):



    user_input = int(input("Enter cm: "))



    print("{} cm is {} inches.".format(user_input, cm_to_inch(user_input)))



if (choice == 2):
```

```python
    user_input = int(input("Enter inches: "))



    print("{} inches is {} cm.".format(user_input, inch_to_cm(user_input)))



print("Thank you for using the program.")
```

Homework program:

- Convert the programs you have already made to use UDFs

Classes

Classes are a feature of Python that bring it more in line with some of the more difficult programming languages. They are essentially "programs within programs" because of how many features you can put into one. Moreover, it is good programming form to use classes for organization. Object-oriented languages such as Python occasionally show their object roots through concepts like these, whereas objects contain attributes in the form "object.attribute". See the example below to understand.

```
class student:


    def __init__(self, name, grade):
```

```
self.name = name

self.grade = grade

self.gpa = 0.0
```

The class that we create is called "student", and student contains its own variables. Classes give us a way to organize objects and give them personal attributes. So instead of having student1_name, student1_grade, student2_grade, etc... as different variables, they can be consolidated by belonging to a class. Within a program, the class declaration goes at the very top. Just like a UDF, it does not actually run in the main program until called.

```
student1 = student("Tim", "Freshman")
#object is student1, an attribute is
"name".
```

Our newly declared "student" class is used to create the student1 object with the attributes "Tim" and "Freshman". This would have previously taken two lines, but it is condensed considerably with classes. Classes compartmentalize the related variables of the object so that each "student" declared has the 3 properties "name", "grade", and "gpa". The second line of our class declaration contains __init__, which is a "method" (user defined function) that runs when an object in the student class is created. Init's parameters are the ones required when creating that object. Self is not actually a parameter, it just refers to "student", but "name" and "grade" are required, which is why we included them when creating "student1". Attributes of student1 can be called like so:

print (student1.name)

Which would simply print "Tim". We did not declare the GPA variable during the student1 initialization, so we can do that with an assignment statement.

student1.gpa = 4.0

Or otherwise change an attribute that already exists.

student1.grade = "Sophomore"

If we were to create another object, it would have its own set of attributes that are completely different from student1.

```
student2 = student("Mary", "Senior")
```

  Where student1.grade is different from student2.grade, even though they share the same variable name. For large projects with multiple repeating variables, classes can reduce the amount of code clutter and variable names to keep track of.

  Looking back to our custom class, we can expand upon it to achieve user defined functions within the class itself.

```
class student:

    def __init__(self, name, grade):
```

```python
        self.name = name

        self.grade = grade

        self.gpa = 0.0


    def record(self):


        return "Student {} is a {} with a
{}".format(self.name, self.grade,
self.gpa)


student3 = student("Lily", "Junior")
```

```
student3.gpa = 3.67
```

```
print (student3.record())
```

The __init__ stays the same, but we add a UDF definition with the name "record". It passes the parameter self (because it has to refer to the class) and returns a formatted string. In our actual main program student3 is created. Finally, we call the UDF with student3.record() (object.function). It returns our formatted string, and therefore it is printed out by print().

Special Methods

The __init__ method is actually a form of a UDF. However, methods that are surrounded by two underscores are special methods within Python, which means they run automatically at certain times. __init__ is a special method also specifically called a "constructor method". Constructor methods get called whenever an object is created, and that is why we put variable declarations within it. When student3 is created, so too are student3.name, student3.grade, and student3.gpa. Therefore, any code that is put within the __init__ block will be activated any time an object is created for the first time.

Other special methods exist, and they are called on different events.

- ___del___ - called whenever an object is deleted (del). Also called destructor method.

- ___str___ - called when an object is passed as a string

- ___setattr___ - will run every time an attribute is set with a value

- ___delattr___ - same as setattr, but only runs when an attribute is deleted

Adding in these special methods can show when they run.

```python
class student:


    def __init__(self, name, grade):


        self.name = name
        self.grade = grade


        self.gpa = 0.0


    def __str__(self):


        return "{}".format(self.name)
```

```python
def record(self):



    return "Student {} is a {} with a
{}".format(self.name, self.grade,
self.gpa)



student4 = student("Barry", "Professor")



print (student4)
```

When student4 is printed
(referenced as a string), the __str__
special method takes over and returns
the "name" attribute of the object. If
this special method was not in there, we
would not get the intended output from
referencing the object.

Finally, classes are useful because we can create "class variables" within them. "Name" and "GPA" are attribute variables that are specific to each object declared, but there can also be class variables that are shared by all objects. For instance, this program will keep track of the total number of objects using a class variable.

```python
class food:


    total_foods = 0


    def __init__(self, name):


        self.name = name
```

```python
        self.calories = 0

        self.foodgroup = ""

        food.total_foods += 1

    def __del__(self):

        food.total_foods -= 1

    def __str__(self):
```

```python
        return "{}".format(self.name)


    def get_total():


        return food.total_foods


    def record(self):


        return "Food {0} is a {2} with {1}
calories.".format(self.name, self.calories,
self.foodgroup)


food1 = food("Carrot Stew")
```

```
food1.calories = 210

food1.foodgroup = "Vegetables"

food2 = food("Buttered Toast")

food2.calories = 100

food2.foodgroup = "Grains"

print (food.get_total())
```

```
del food2
```

```
print (food.get_total())
```

      As the program creates a food, 1 is added to total_foods. Then, a food object is deleted so 1 is taken away. The console prints 2, then 1 to show how our UDF can be called to check the class variable. Keeping track of the number of something is a common use for class variables, but they are highly useful for other situations as well.

Example Program 6 – project6.py

```python
class house:

    def __init__(self, name, bedrooms,
bathrooms, cost):

        self.name = name

        self.bedrooms = bedrooms

        self.bathrooms = bathrooms
```

```python
        self.cost = cost


        print("House for sale!")


    def __del__(self):


        print("House off the market.")


print("House for sale:")


user_input = input("What is the address
of the house? ")
```

```python
user_input2 = int(input("How many
bedrooms? "))


user_input3 = int(input("How many
bathrooms? "))


user_input4 = int(input("How much
does it cost? "))


house1 = house(user_input,
user_input2, user_input3, user_input4)


print("Looking for buyers...")


for x in range (0, house1.cost):
```

```
x += 1 #wait a while
```

```
print("Sold!")
```

```
del house1
```

Homework program:

- Use classes to make a database organization program. Users should be able to create new entries of a class and set variables, and also view them at will.

Inheritance

In your more robust and expansive programs, you might use multiple related classes. As an example, think of the program where you must categorize devices on a network. Each device type (desktop, laptop, phone, etc...) will have its own class, but you will ultimately be repeating commonly used attributes. Both desktops and laptops will have names, departments, and IP addresses, but they will also have a few distinct variables specific to them such as Wi-Fi for the laptops and graphics cards for the desktop.

Through a process called "inheritance", classes can be put into a parent/child relationship where certain parent attributes can be "inherited" by children classes. Effectively sharing attributes across classes leads to more elegant organization and less code overall.

```python
class device:


    total_devices = 0


    def __init__(self, name, owner):


        self.name = name


        self.owner = owner


        device.total_devices += 1
```

```python
    def __del__(self):


        device.total_devices -= 1


    def __str__(self):


        return "{}".format(self.name)


    def get_total():


        return device.total_devices
```

```python
class laptop(device):

    def __init__(self, name, owner, wifi):

        device.__init__(self, name, owner)
        self.wifi = wifi

    def __str__(self):

        return "{} is owned by {} and connected to {}".format(self.name, self.owner, self.wifi)

class cellular(device):
```

```python
    def __init__(self, name, owner,
connection, BYOD):


        device.__init__(self, name, owner)


        self.connection = connection


        self.BYOD = BYOD


    def __str__(self):


        return "{} is owned by {} and it uses
{}.  BYOD? {}".format(self.name,
self.owner, self.connection, self.BYOD)
```

```python
device1 = laptop("STAFF12", "IT",
"Staff-wifi")


device2 = cellular("Jack's-iDevice",
"Jack", "4G LTE", "yes")


print (device1)


print (device2)


print (device.get_total())
```

In this program, the parent class "device" is created with 2 attributes – name and owner. The other classes, laptop and cellular, also contain name and owner attributes, so we set them up to inherit them from the parent class. To set a class into a parent/child relationship, the child class must pass the parent class as a parameter in the declaration. This is why "class cellular(device)" is used, because we are setting cellular to be linked to device.

Secondly, we call the device constructor method specifically within each child class constructor method. When this is done, the child class actually runs the entire parent constructor method. Name and owner are obtained this way, and also the "total_devices += 1" line gets passed as well.

Both children contain a __str__ method, even though the parent class also has one. Through a process called overwriting, if a special method is called that exists in both the parent and child, than only the child method will run. In the absence of a called method in a child, the parent will runs its method instead. This is why referencing a laptop object as a string will display laptop information, but deleting a laptop object will fall back to the parent and run its destructor method instead.

Understanding how inheritance works can provide your applications with unprecedented organization and composition. Most higher-level and advanced programs take advantage of classes and their properties to quickly devise a framework for many applications such as database tools, so learning them would undoubtedly improve your Python skills.

Example Program 7 – project7.py

```python
class house:


    def __init__(self, name, bedrooms, bathrooms):


        self.name = name


        self.bedrooms = bedrooms


        self.bathrooms = bathrooms
```

```python
        self.cost = 0


        print("Living space for sale!")


    def __del__(self):


        print("Living space off the market.")


class apartment(house):


    def __init__(self, name, bedrooms,
bathrooms):
```

```
house.__init__(self, name,
bedrooms, bathrooms)
```

```
self.montly_payment = 0
```

```
forsale1 = apartment("100 Col. Ave", 2,
2)
```

```
forsale1.montly_payment = 250
```

Homework program:

- Expand the database program that you could optionally create in the last chapter to include inheritance.

Modules

Every bit of functionality that we have used so far is built-in to Python already. Python is an expansive language, but additional features can be added to Python easily through modules. Those familiar with C can relate modules to "h" files and preprocessor statements. Modules do much the same thing, they are included in order to add new functions and commands to Python.

To add a new module, we only need to include one statement at the top of our program.

```
import math
```

So in this line, we import the "math" module, which opens up a slew of new functions for us to use.

```python
import math


print (math.sin(3))


answer = math.sqrt(16)


print (answer)


print (math.gcd(100, 125))
```

In particular, sqrt(), sin(), and gcd() are three examples you can notice above. Every module has a defined purpose, and math's is to provide advanced mathematical functions. Here is a list of the most important ones.

- math.sqrt() – square root of number

- math.sin() – sine of number

- math.cos() – cosine of number

- math.tan() – tangent of number

- math.log() – two parameters, log and base

- math.pi – 3.14159

- math.e – 2.71828

Those needing to use complicated functions such as the ones above only need to "import math" at the top of the program.

Other specialized modules exist as well, such as datetime. Datetime is a module that provides time-keeping functions.

```
import datetime
```

```
current_time =
datetime.datetime.now()
```

```
print (current_time.hour)
```

```
print (current_time.minute)
```

```
print (current_time.second)
```

Other functions provided through datetime include:

- year
- month
- day

Or os, a module that unlocks operating system functions for altering files. Here is a small program for creating a new folder and then making it the active directory.

import os

os.mkdir("folder") #make folder

os.chdir("folder") #go into folder

os.chdir("..") #up one directory

More functions available to os are listed.

- os.rmdir() – delete specified folder

- os.remove() – delete specified file

- os.path.exists() – checks to see if specified file exists

- os.rename() – renames specified file to second parameter supplied

And other highly useful modules, such as random, statistics, and pip exist that can give new features to your Python applications that were not previously possible. Python also has support for downloading and using user-created modules, but that is an advanced concept not covered here.

Example Program 8 – project8.py

```
import random


print ("Fortune telling...")


rng = random.randrange(1, 7)


if (rng == 1):


    print("You will soon come into
money.")
```

```python
elif (rng == 2):


    print("Consider buying stocks.")


elif (rng == 3):


    print("Look both ways before
crossing.")


elif (rng == 4):


    print("Call your relatives...")
```

```python
elif (rng == 5):



    print("You will get a phone call.")
else:



    print("Future cloudy... Try again.")
```

Homework project:

- Create a "sampler" program that shows off various Python module features.

Common Errors

Because many programmers choose Python as their first language to learn, they often succumb to a few common errors. If your applications are not functioning correctly, or if you are looking for a few of the best programming practices, than this section will help you. When code is run through Python, it may stop and return an error to you. By reading the error you can learn which line the error comes from, and usually Python will point (^) to the exact character that is wrong. Use the information that is given to you to understand your error and rectify the situation.

Not specifying the correct parameters is a common newbie mistake. When putting values between the parentheses for a function, you must pay close attention to what kind of data it expects. Some functions require only integers, and some have 2 or more parameters to enter. When in doubt, consult the Python documentation page for the specific function you are working with. Advanced IDEs, such as Atom and Eclipse often are programmed to display an example parameter list as you are typing out a function, and you can follow along with the example to know what each parameter is expecting.

Sometimes we forget to convert user input to an integer. If we are prompting a user for numerical input, we must surround input() with int() for float(). Failure to do this will pass the input as a string, which will likely return an error.

When comparing two values, Python requires the programmer to use the double equal sign (==). When assigning a value, you must use the single equal sign (=). Using an inappropriate sign for any occasion will always return a syntax error.

After every comparison statement and loop (such as if, elif, else, for, while, def, and class) there is a colon (:). This colon denotes that the next line should be indented, and thus all indented lines will fall within the function's scope. Failure to place a colon returns a syntax error.

Strings and functions are usually surrounded by a pair of characters. Functions use parentheses, while strings use quotations to indicate where their boundaries are. If you ever forget to supply the closing character, Python will surely return an error.

Beginners will often try to use functions that are not in Python by default without including the correct module. Trying to call an advanced math function, or editing a file directory is not possible with regular Python. Always place the import commands for modules you will use at the top of the program, or the application will simply not run.

Indentations are required in Python. Those coming from other programming languages will likely forget this and indent in their own personal style. This will break mostly all Python programs, because the interpreter expects a certain formatting standard. An error will be returned every time that indentations are incorrect. Pay close attention to your indentation levels or risk your program failing to logic and syntax errors.

Programming languages demand perfect syntax at all times. Because of this, even a spelling error can be disastrous for our applications. Besides indentation problems and misspelled functions, giving the wrong variable name or accidentally calling the wrong function can make your program fail outright or perform unexpectedly. When coding, double check over your scripts to ensure no characters are out of place. Test your code after each implementation so you know that when an error occurs it should be coming from a new addition. Sometimes there is an error or bug in the code and it just cannot be rectified after reviewing the code. Programmers must "debug" their code by following it line-by-line at this point, "tracing" the path that the interpreter takes as it runs the program. Some IDE's have tools for debugging, such as "breakpoints" or "line stops" that allow you to run each line at the click of a button. Taking the program slow like that can reveal the source of the issue most of the time, but it takes a keen eye and a dedicated troubleshooter to fix code.

Many programmers consider it unnecessary, but commenting your scripts is an essential part of coding. Failure to do so is an extremely common beginner mistake that many first time programmers fall for. Once you master the art of Python and begin programming in a company with other coders, there might be multiple people working on the same script. Even the cleanest code is confusing to look at for the first time, but comments help to demystify the complex characters. Moreover, coming back to an old script of yours from weeks past can feel like reading a foreign language- comments help you to quickly get back to coding. Many programmers put a comment as the top line of their program with a brief description of what the script does, when it was written, and any contributors to it. That way the next time you are quickly looking through files trying to find a certain program, the comments can help you understand what is inside without actually running or deciphering the code.

The final common mistake that runs rampant in Python newbies is variable naming. If it has not already been brought to light in your experimentation, there are just certain names that you cannot name your variables. "Reserved" words such as class, break, print, and, or, while, etc... are keywords that cannot be used for a variable name. If Python detects their use a syntax error will occur. Besides errors, though, programmers often use bad form when naming their variables. Avoid ambiguous and simple variable names such as "number" or "var1" in favor of descriptive one such as "user_input" or "totalNumberOfDogs". These variables explain their use at a glance, so a verbose programmer will never misuse a variable or have to check what its intent is. Python programmers typically use the underscore method to name their variables (grade_average, dog_1), but camelCase is acceptable as well (userInput, multAnswer). No matter which method is used, a skillful programmer will always make the name descriptive.

Conclusion

Thank you again for downloading this beginner's guide to Python. Now that you have finished the text, you have a basic knowledge of how Python works, and you should be able to write your own programs. You can further increase your knowledge by attempting to create larger and more complicated programs, or you can study modules and learn new functions. If you have enjoyed the book, rate and leave a review on Amazon so more high quality books can be produced.

Related Titles

[Hacking University: Freshman Edition Essential Beginner's Guide on How to Become an Amateur Hacker](#)

Hacking University: Sophomore Edition. Essential Guide to Take Your Hacking Skills to the Next Level. Hacking Mobile Devices, Tablets, Game Consoles, and Apps

Hacking University: Junior Edition.
Learn Python Computer Programming
From Scratch. Become a Python Zero to
Hero. The Ultimate Beginners Guide in
Mastering the Python Language

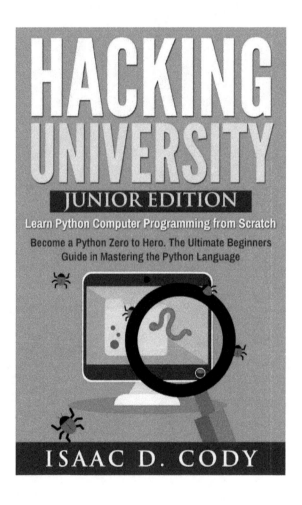

Hacking University: Senior Edition
Linux. Optimal Beginner's Guide To
Precisely Learn And Conquer The Linux
Operating System. A Complete Step By
Step Guide In How Linux Command
Line Works

Hacking University: Graduation Edition. 4 Manuscripts (Computer, Mobile, Python, & Linux). Hacking Computers, Mobile Devices, Apps, Game Consoles and Learn Python & Linux

Data Analytics: Practical Data Analysis and Statistical Guide to Transform and Evolve Any Business, Leveraging the power of Data Analytics, Data Science, and Predictive Analytics for Beginners

About the Author

Isaac D. Cody is a proud, savvy, and ethical hacker from New York City. After receiving a Bachelors of Science at Syracuse University, Isaac now works for a mid-size Informational Technology Firm in the heart of NYC. He aspires to work for the United States government as a security hacker, but also loves teaching others about the future of technology. Isaac firmly believes that the future will heavily rely computer "geeks" for both security and the successes of companies and future jobs alike. In his spare time, he loves to analyze and scrutinize everything about the game of basketball.